to play and sing

And
Christ
became a
human being and
lived here on earth
among us and was full of
loving forgiveness and truth.
And some of us have seen His glory,
the glory of the only Son of the heavenly Father! . . . This was how the birth of Jesus took place.
His mother Mary was engaged to Joseph, but before they were married, she found out that
she was going to have a baby by the Holy Spirit. This happened in order to make what the
Lord had said through the prophet come true, "A virgin will become pregnant and have a
son, and he will be called 'Immanuel' (which means 'God is with us')" . . . At that time the
Emperor Augustus ordered a census to be taken throughout the Roman Empire. Joseph
went from the town of Nazareth in Galilee to the town of Bethlehem in Judea, the birthplace
of King David . . . While they were there the time came for Mary's baby to be born. She
gave birth to her first son, wrapped him in strips of cloth and laid him in a manger
because there was no room for them to stay in the inn . . . That night some shepherds
were in the fields outside the village. Suddenly an angel appeared among them and
said "Don't be afraid! I bring you the most joyful news ever announced, and it is for
everyone! The Saviour - yes, the Messiah, the Lord - has been born tonight in Bethlehem!"
They ran to the village and found their way to Mary and Joseph. And there was the baby, lying in
the manger just as the angel had told them. All who heard the shepherds' story were amazed at what
they said. Mary quietly treasured these things in her heart and often thought about them. The shepherds
went back, praising God for all they had heard and seen . . . Soon afterwards, some men who studied the stars
came from the east to Jerusalem and asked, "Where is the baby born to be King of the Jews? We saw his star come
up in the east, and we have come to worship Him." The star went ahead of them until it stopped over the place
where the child was. When they saw the child with his mother Mary, they knelt and worshipped Him.
They brought out their gifts of gold, frankincense and myrrh, and presented them to Him.
Then they returned to their own country by another road since God had warned
them in a dream not to return to Herod in Jerusalem . . . For God loved
the world so much that He gave His only Son, so that everyone who
believes in Him may not die but have eternal life . . . And these
things have been written that you may believe that Jesus is the
Messiah, the Son of God, and that through your faith in Him you
may have life . . . and so we sing with all the angels - 'Glory to
God in highest heaven and peace on earth to all mankind.'
alleluia, alleluia, alleluia,   alleluia, alleluia, alleluia,
alleluia, alleluia,   alleluia, alleluia,
alleluia,   alleluia,
Amen   Amen

David and Christa Liggins

Ocarina Carols to play and sing	ISBN 1 871210 09 7
'Play your ocarina' - Books 1 to 4 - Complete guide (128 pp)	ISBN 1 871210 08 9
Book 1 Starting off - basic skills and tunes	ISBN 1 871210 04 6
Book 2 Moving on - further technique and tunes	ISBN 1 871210 05 4
Book 3 Going for it - solos and duets	ISBN 1 871210 06 2
Book 4 Finishing touches - extending your repertoire	ISBN 1 871210 07 0

Ocarina Workshop Publications

Before playing your ocarina, remember:

- Always wear the ocarina round your neck
- Support your ocarina with 3rd and 4th fingers above and below the string-end
- Breathe steadily to produce your best sound, tilting the string-end down
- Tongue notes for a clear sound - see 'Play your ocarina' books for tuition

Ocarina notation

Scale of 'D' major

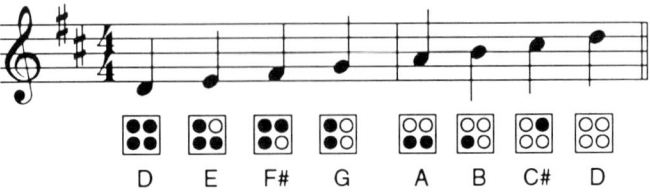

A full chromatic scale appears inside the back cover

4-hole and 6-hole ocarina playing

- All carols in this collection can be played on both 4-hole and 6-hole ocarinas
- On 4-hole ocarinas, substitute suggested alternative notes when they appear
- On 6-hole ocarinas, cover thumb-holes unless charts show them open
- Open the left thumb-hole when playing top 'D' (see above) for best tuning
- ② and ③ opposite refer to carols arranged with optional harmony parts

Carols

Ocarina Carols

Christmas is full of activity - wrapping presents, sending cards and decorating trees. The first Christmas was equally full of activity as shepherds watched and wondered, wise men travelled and Mary produced!

In all this activity, there has always been great singing and celebration with shepherds, wise men and generations of worshippers echoing the song of the angels:

'Glory to God in the highest - and on earth, peace, good will toward all mankind'.

The idea of singing at Christmas is not a new one but 'ocarina playing' can give a new slant to old festivities. Young and old alike are able to play together, sharing the familiar story through the very best of music and words, written over many centuries. Anyone with a little skill and practice will also find they can soon play carols well enough to give their first public performance. This may be in a Christmas concert, at a family gathering or with groups of carol singers in the street. Keep your ocarina warm if playing in cold conditions! Give it an occasional 'hot blast', covering the whistle-hole with your finger.

We wish you a very merry Christmas and hope that the joy and peace of this special time of year may be yours as you breathe life into the words and music of this book.

Contents

As with gladness ③	24	Joy to the world	29
Away in a manger	19	Mary had a baby ③	25
Angels from the realms of glory	21	O come, all ye faithful	7
Boar's head carol ③	26	O little town of Bethlehem ②	16
Deck the hall	28	Once in royal David's city	6
Ding dong! merrily on high	22	See, amid the winter's snow	5
Gloucestershire wassail	31	Silent night	18
God rest you merry, gentlemen	15	The first Nowell ②	8
Good King Wenceslas	4	The holly and the ivy	30
Hark! the herald angels sing	14	We three kings	13
I saw three ships	12	We wish you a merry Christmas	32
In the bleak mid-winter ②	17	While shepherds watched ②	23
It came upon the midnight clear	20	While shepherds watched ③	27
Jingle bells ②	10	Words to 'Ocarina Carols'	centre

Carols 3

Good King Wenceslas

See, amid the winter's snow

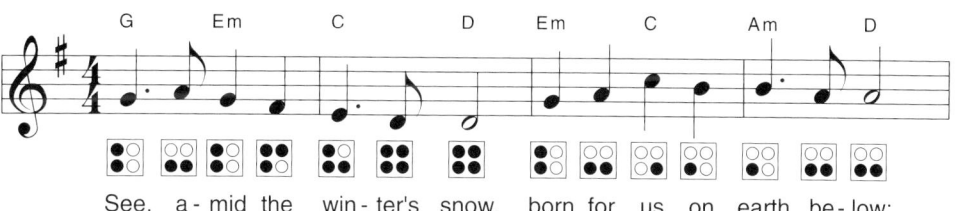

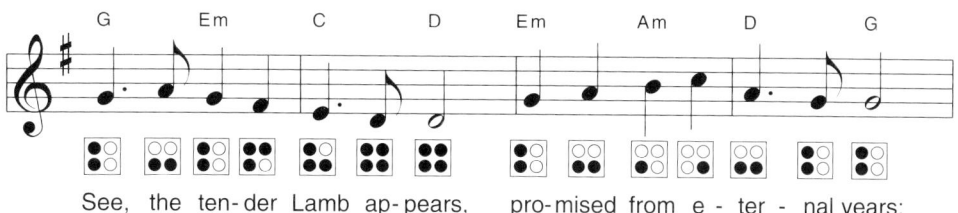

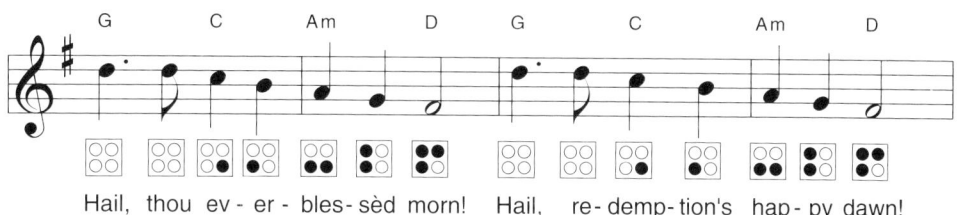

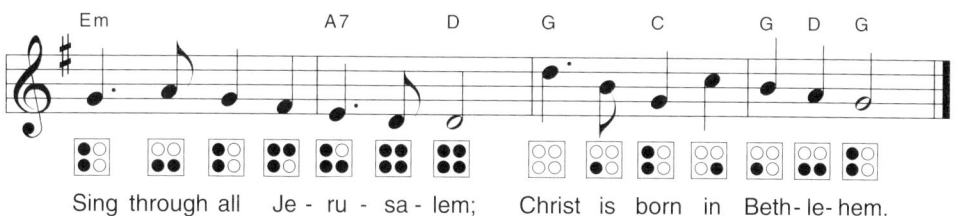

Carols

Once in royal David's city

Carols

O come, all ye faithful

Carols

The first Nowell

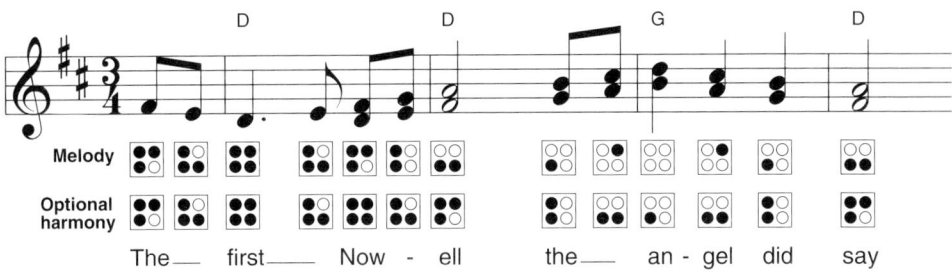

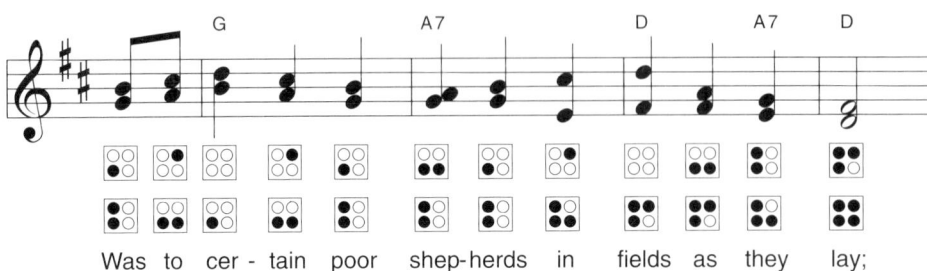

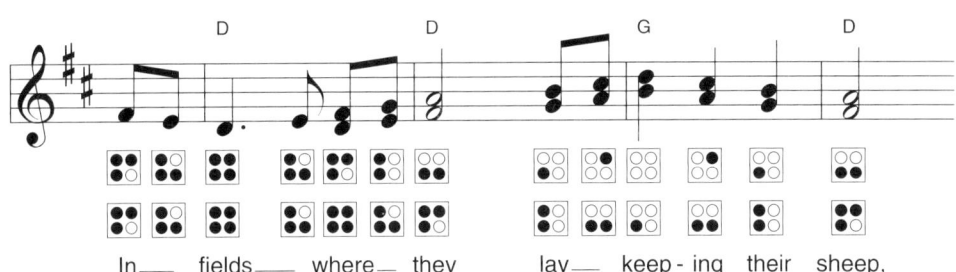

This is the first of five 'Ocarina Carol' duets. Play the melody by itself, either on your own or in unison with others. Add the harmony when you are ready. Select ocarinas of the same size or in the same key an octave apart.

Carols

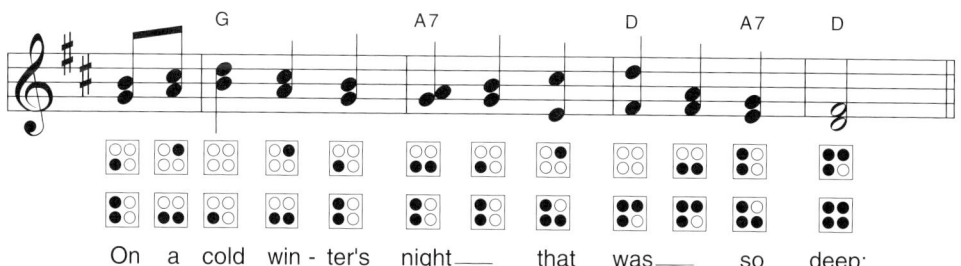

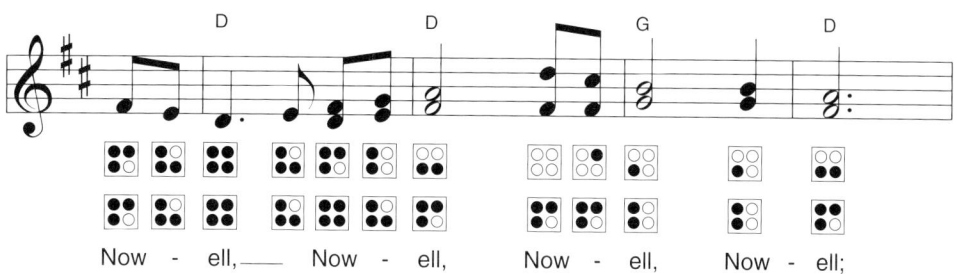

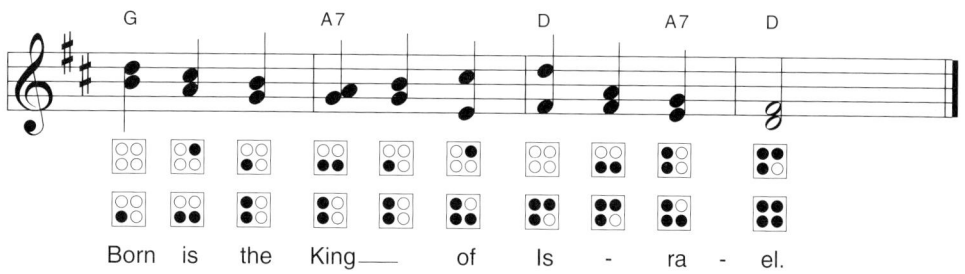

Sing the words to discover the rhythm of the music. In 'The first Nowell', both melody and harmony move together. Look out for harmonies moving unexpectedly elsewhere! (See 'Jingle Bells' overleaf.)

Carols

Jingle bells

Carols

Carols

I saw three ships

First tune

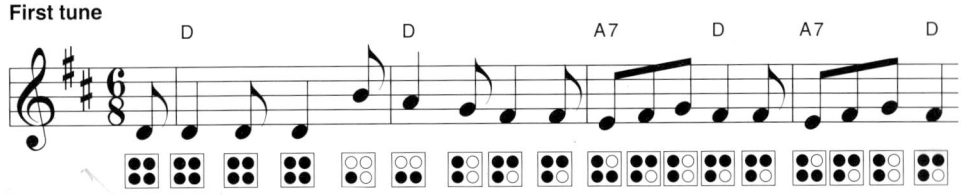

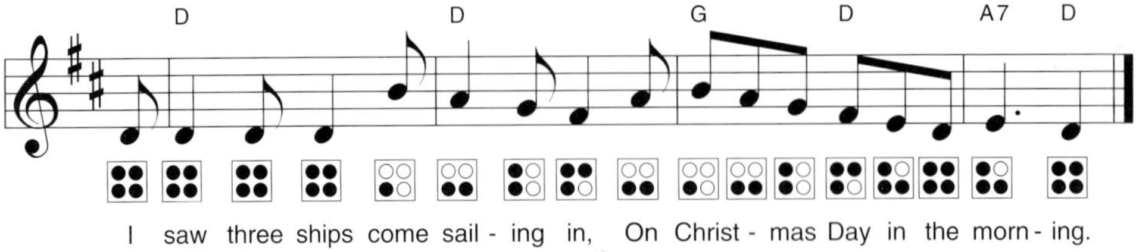

Second tune

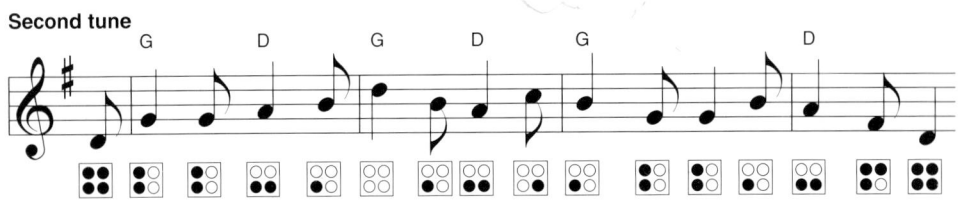

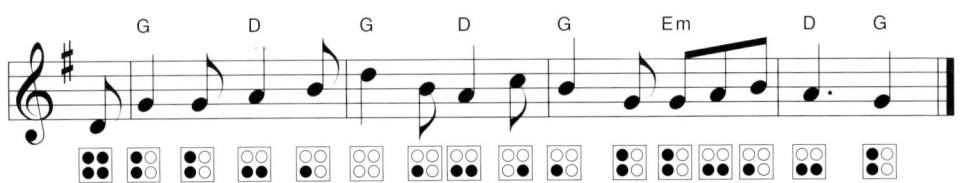

Choose just one tune for 'I saw three ships'. Play all three tunes on these pages, one after another, to make a strong instrumental medley with interesting changes of key.

Carols

We three kings

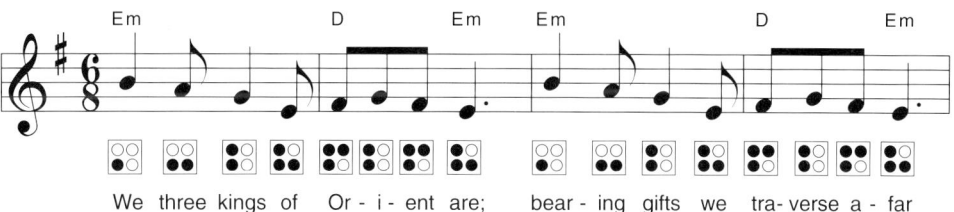

We three kings of Or - i - ent are; bear - ing gifts we tra - verse a - far

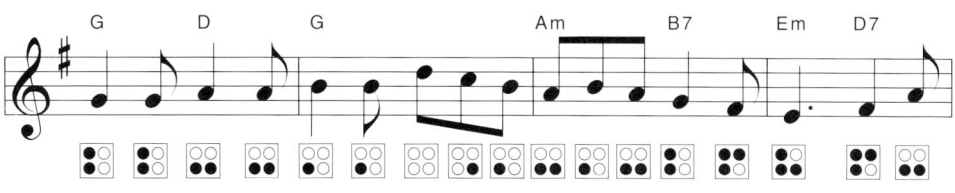

Field and foun - tain, moor and moun - tain, fol - low - ing yon - der star: O —

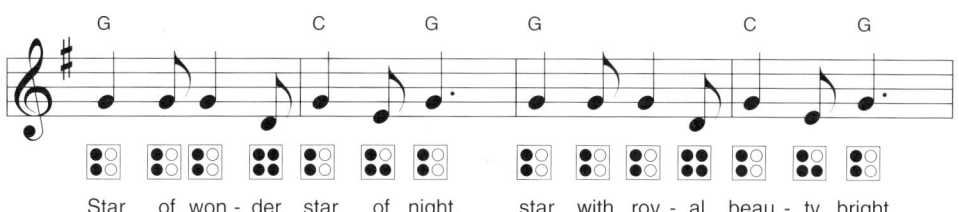

Star of won - der, star of night, star with roy - al beau - ty bright,

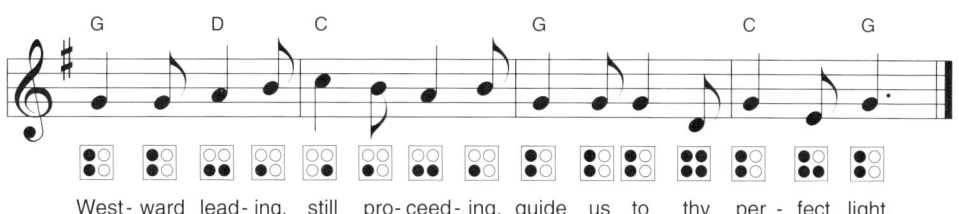

West - ward lead - ing, still pro - ceed - ing, guide us to thy per - fect light.

As you sing and play through this book, add other instruments if you have them. Guitar chords give ideas for further harmonies.

Carols

God rest you merry, gentlemen

Carols

arrangement copyright © 1994 Ocarina Workshop Publications - copying prohibited

O little town of Bethlehem

16 arrangement copyright © 1994 Ocarina Workshop Publications - copying prohibited   Carols

In the bleak mid-winter

Carols   arrangement copyright © 1994 Ocarina Workshop Publications - copying prohibited   17

Silent night

18   Carols

Away in a manger

Carols   arrangement copyright © 1994 Ocarina Workshop Publications - copying prohibited

It came upon the midnight clear

Carols

Angels from the realms of glory

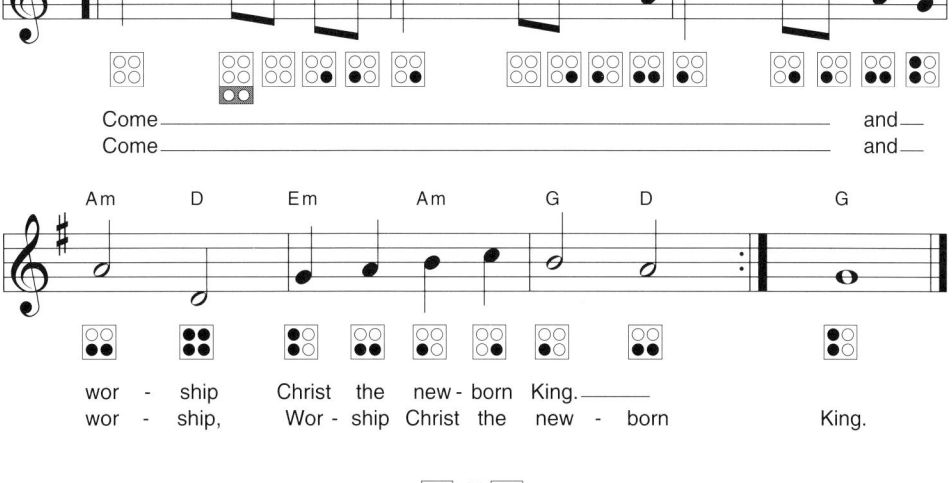

Carols

Ding dong! merrily on high

Carols

While shepherds watched

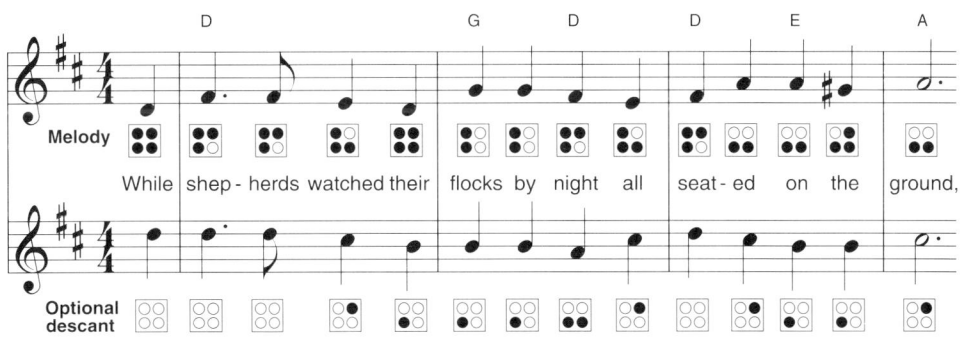

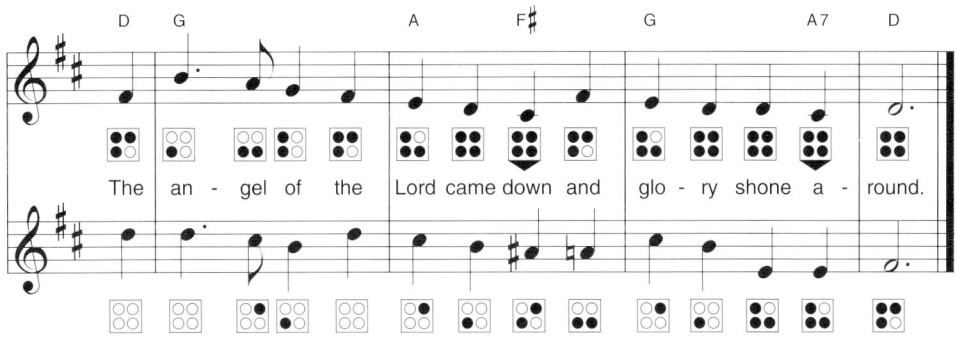

The descant on this page is the only harmony in 'Ocarina Carols' which is written to play or sing at a higher pitch than the melody. It may also be played on a larger instrument an octave lower as a bass accompaniment.

Guitar chords above and on the next two pages should only be used when the melody is played in unison. The richness of the harmony parts is best heard unaccompanied.

The following four pages are all arranged for two ocarinas at the same pitch with a third instrument an octave below. We recommend two Alto ocarinas with a Bass.

Try the various arrangements with groups of ocarinas on each part. Large numbers of ocarinas playing descants and harmonies give a 'lift' to the singing of any carol.

'Mary had a baby' (page 25) line 2 or and line 3 or

Carols   arrangement copyright © 1994 Ocarina Workshop Publications - copying prohibited   **23**

As with gladness

Mary had a baby

Boar's head carol

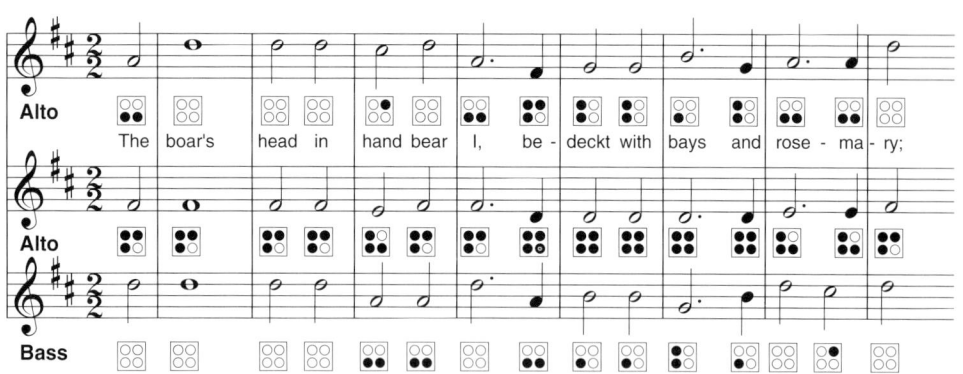
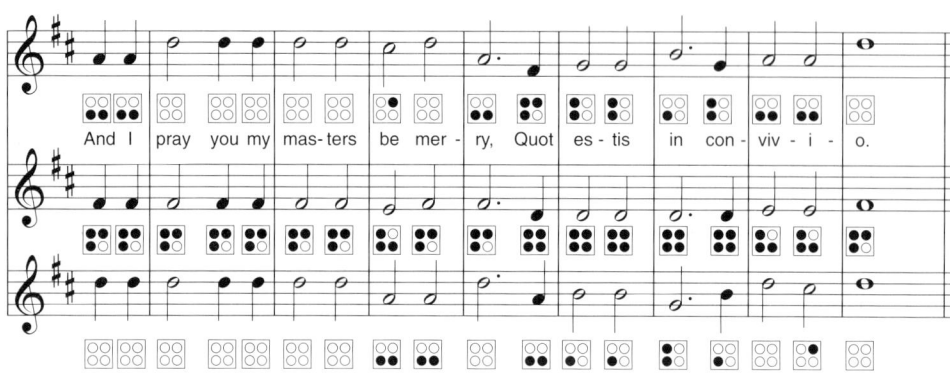
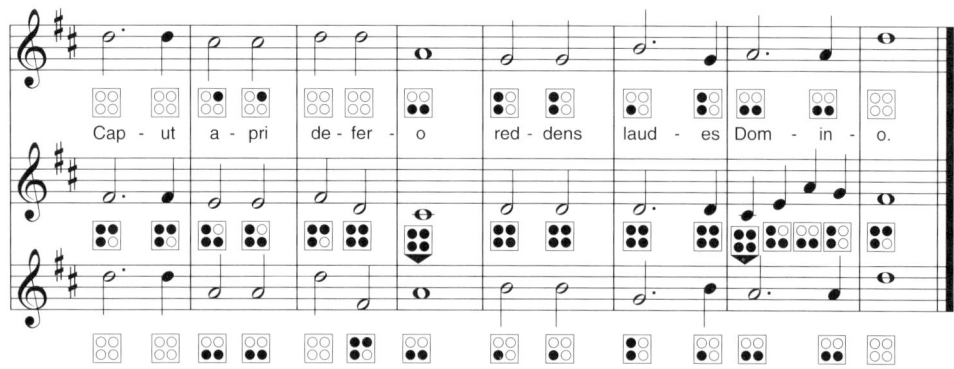

Carols

While shepherds watched

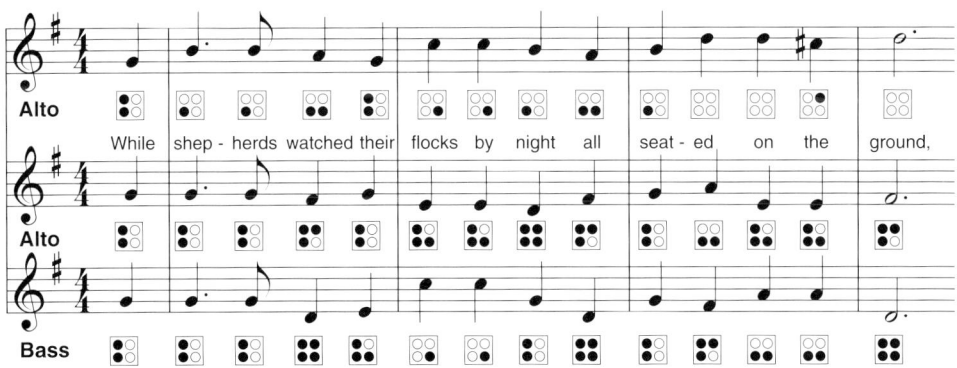

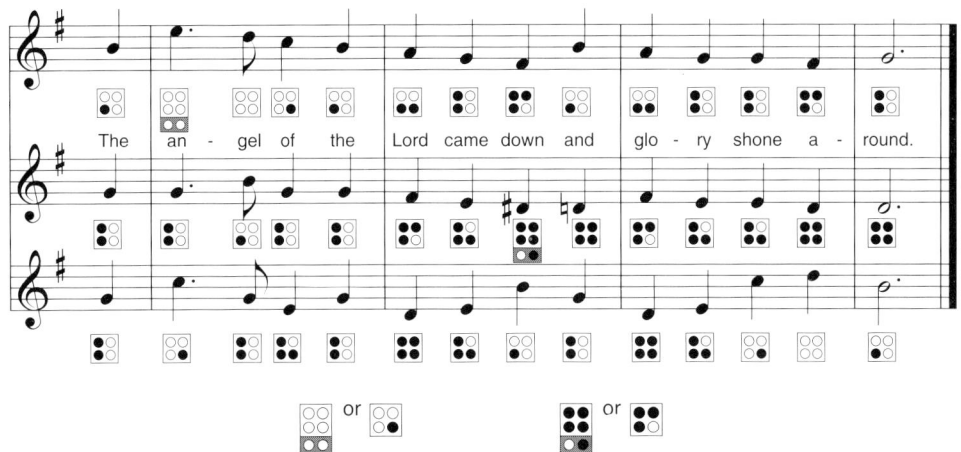

> The 'Boar's head carol' is sung each Christmas Day as the traditional dish is carried in at Queens College, Oxford. It appeared in the first printed carol collection (published 1552).
>
> If you think that's old, the tune to 'Good King Wenceslas' was common in the thirteenth century as a Spring carol ('Tempus adest floridum') celebrating budding trees, growing flowers and lengthening days! Various 'carols' were once sung and danced at all the main festivals including May Day, Easter and New Year.
>
> Christmas carols are popular all over the world. We include 'Silent night' ('Stille Nacht'), 'We three Kings' from the USA and, from the West Indies, 'Mary had a baby'.

Carols   arrangement copyright © 1994 Ocarina Workshop Publications - copying prohibited

Deck the hall

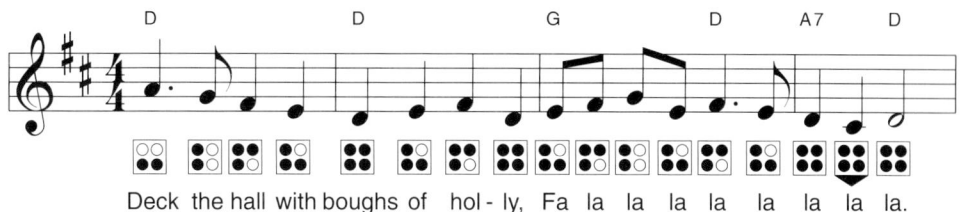
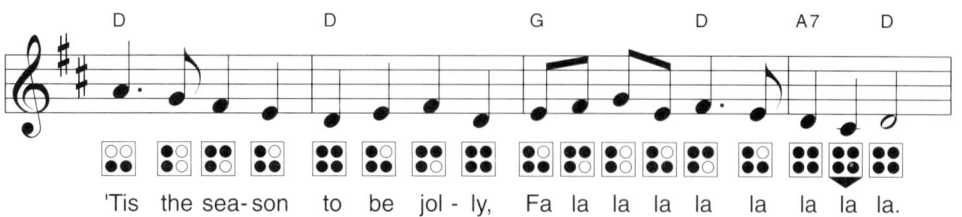
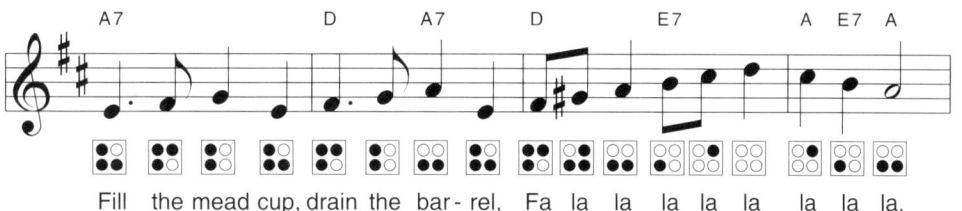
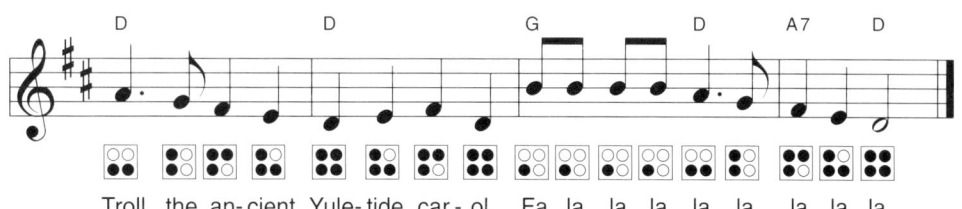

Joy to the world

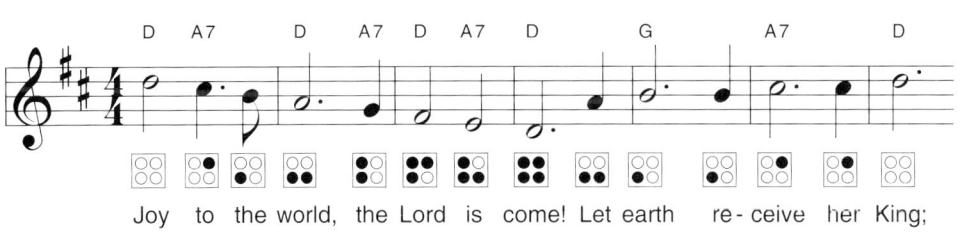
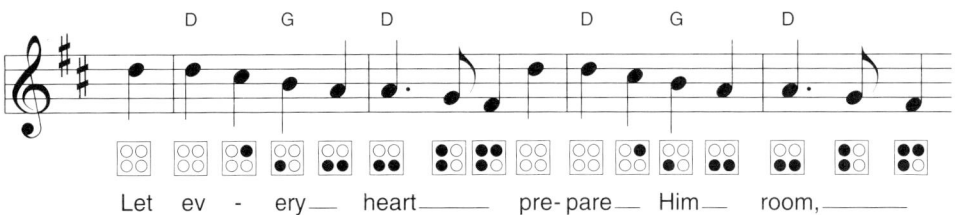
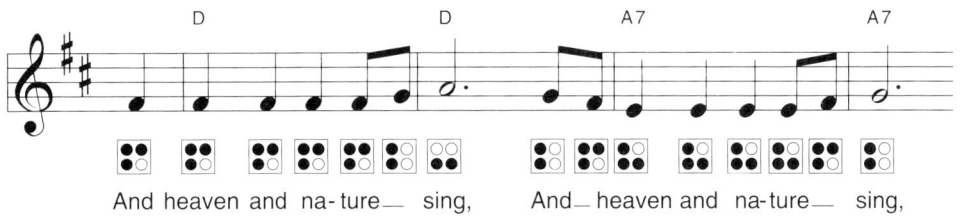
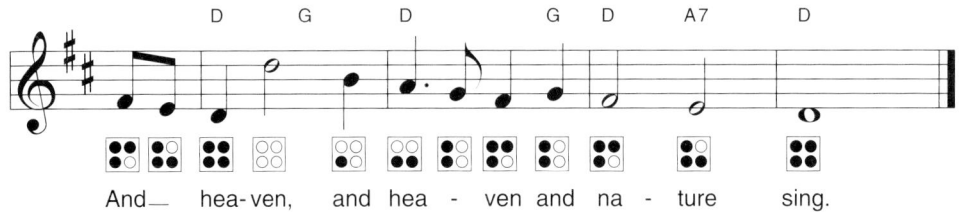

Carols

The holly and the ivy

Carols

Gloucestershire wassail

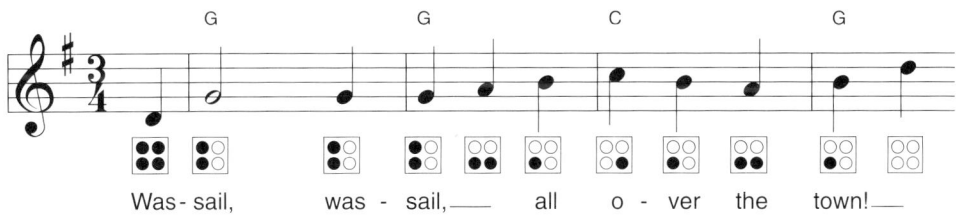
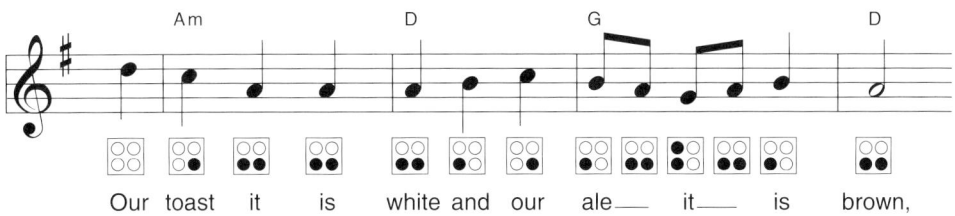
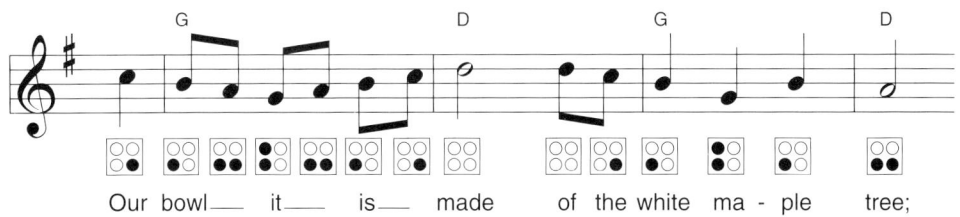
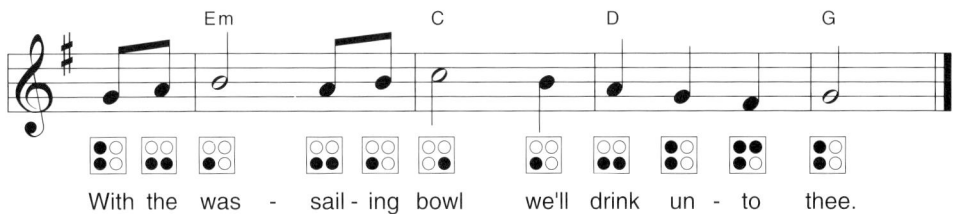

Carols

We wish you a merry Christmas

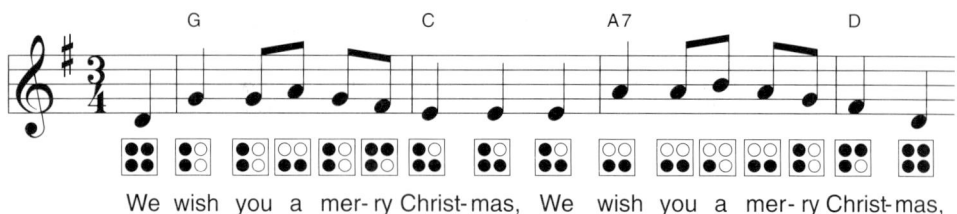
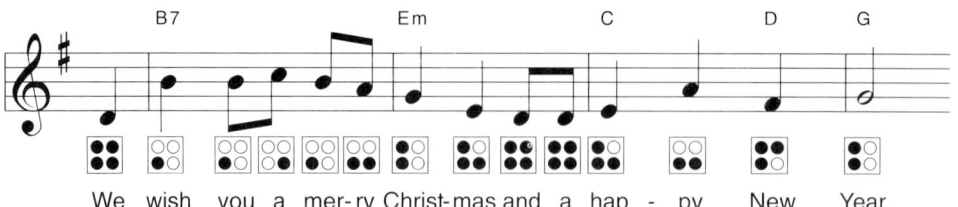
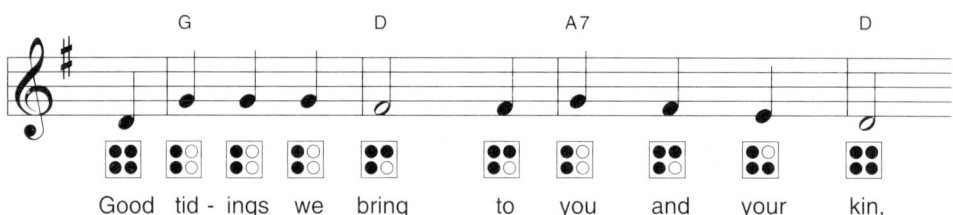
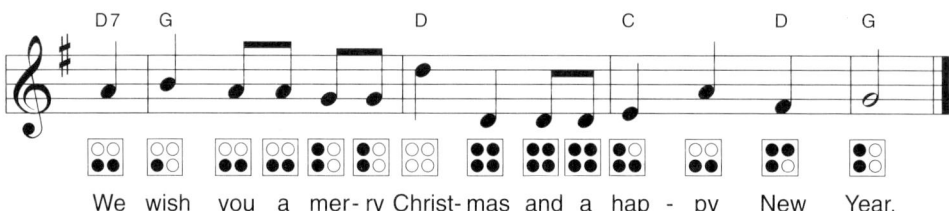

Carols